The Mango's Grace

A kids Yoga & Mindfulness book

Swaady Martin
Illustrated by Yogesh Mahajan

LovingKindness
BOMA

Happy, Loving, Kind and Serene little humans

Conscious values ° Mindfulness ° Diversity ° Positive Messaging

Published by LovingKindness Boma
22 rue Norvins, 75018 Paris, FRANCE
explore@shiftwithin.me
www.lovingkindnessboma.com

Illustrations & Design by Yogesh Mahajan
www.animationwalayogi.in

ISBN Print: 978-2-491573-09-6
ISBN Ebook: 978-2-491573-10-2

Ordering Information:
Quantity sales: Special discounts are available on quantity purchases

by corporations, associations, and others.
For details, please contact the publisher at the email above.

In honor, gratitude and celebration
of our beloved Mother Earth.
We and Earth are One.

Blessings,
Swaady

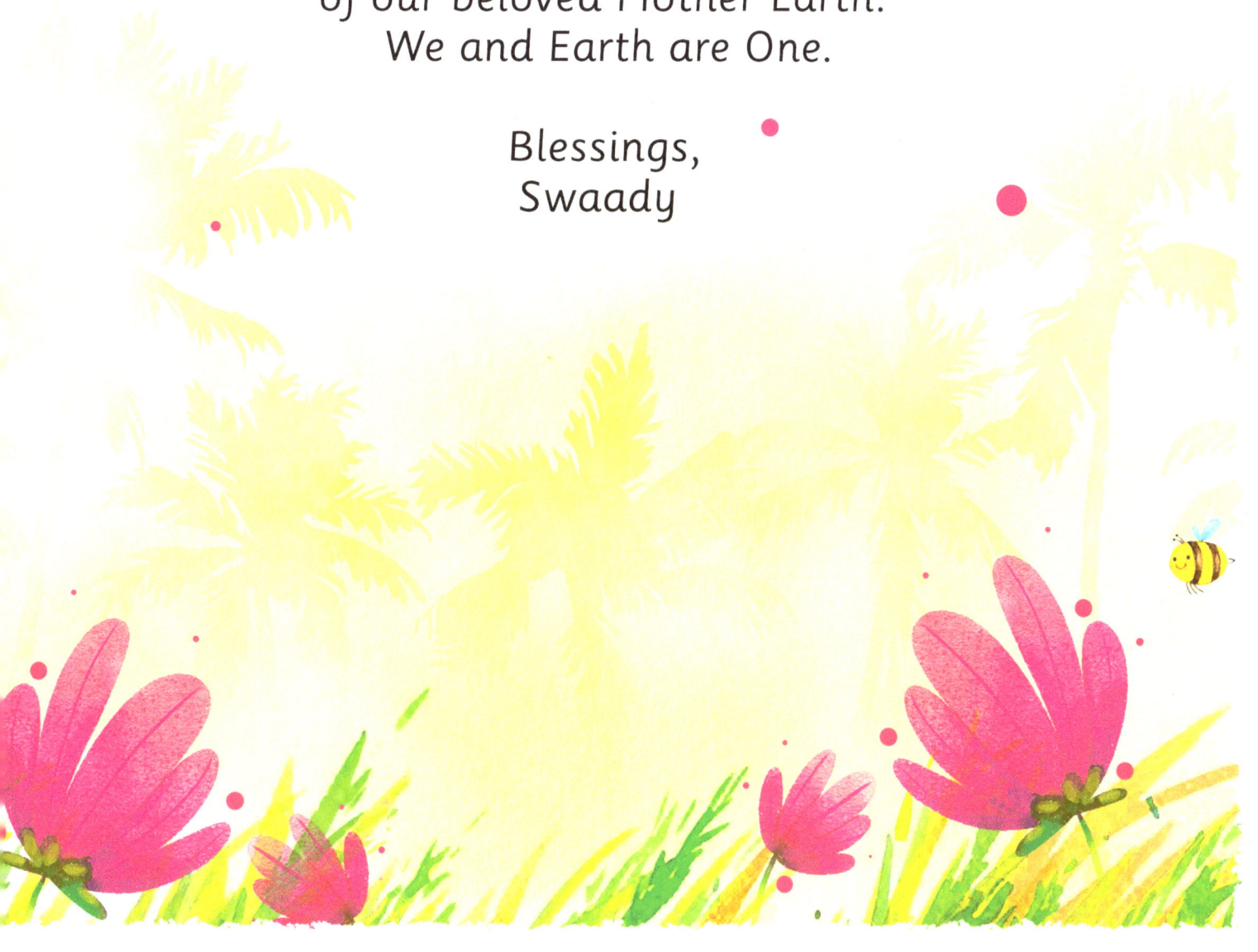

Mokili liked to wander through the tropical food forest with his cat Mbuma.

He would find a cool, shaded spot and sit with a straight back and his legs crossed on the spongy grass of the woodland floor.

The back of his hands would softly rest on his knees as he closed his eyes and opened his palms up to the sun.

Then he would visualize the earth beneath him as a giant cloud floating over the lush ground.

In his mind the cloud would lift and lift and lift,
high into the sky and then drift over the
edible green forest below.

As Mokili was floating through his imagination,
a ladybird landed delicately on his nose.
Mokili wanted to move the ladybird off his face without
hurting her, so he took a long, deep breath.

1, 2, 3 in and then he slowly exhaled. 1, 2, 3 out.

The ladybird did not move so he did it again.

1, 2, 3 in. 1, 2, 3 out.

The ladybird was still here!

He took another long, deep breath.

1, 2, 3 in. And he slowly exhaled. 1, 2, 3.

Finally, the ladybird flapped her wings and flew
away.

Mokili stood up, shaking his legs and arms to wake them.

Shake, shake.

First one leg and then the other.

He twisted his waist then rolled his shoulders and head.

As he moved, a group of frogs jumped towards him. Hop! Hop! Hop! Mokili joined them and connected to the earth with all his senses.

He savored the sounds, the colors and the moist soil under his bare feet.

Imagining a bright sun shining from his heart, Mokili inhaled the rich scent of frangipani flowers. He swept his arms to the sky as if to hold the sun in his hands then looked up.

He said: "Thank you beautiful sun for lighting my day".

While he exhaled Mokili folded his body forwards to reach his toes and said: "Thank you beautiful earth for nourishing me".

As he inhaled once more Mokili bent his knees and placed his palms flat on the moss of the forest floor. He stretched his right leg back into a lunge and looked up. "Thank you beautiful air for my breath"

As if to imitate the log on which Mbuma was relaxing, Mokili held his breath and extended his left leg back to meet the right in a plank. "Thank you beautiful wood for your warming fire."

Then he exhaled and gently lowered his knees, chest and chin onto the moist grass. He saw his reflection in the drops of dew on the blades of grass and exhaled as he said:

"Thank you beautiful water for refreshing and cleansing me."

Inhaling once more, Mokili dropped the tops of his feet onto the ground, stretched his legs back and lifted his heart to the sky. A gentle breeze passed over his cheeks and he said "Thank you beautiful wind for cooling me when I'm hot."

Exhaling, he pushed his hips up and back with the soles of his feet planted firmly on the ground so that he resembled an anthill.

"Thank you Mbuma and all beautiful animals for being such great teachers and for preserving the earth's balance."

nhaling, he moved his right foot forward so that it rested
between his hands. "Thank you beautiful plants for your
medicine."

Exhaling, Mokili brought his left foot forward and bent over
his knees while he said: "Thank you beautiful crystals
and stone beings for your wisdom and healing."

Inhaling, he lifted his arms to the sky again. "Thank you beautiful moon for watching over me at night."

Slowly exhaling, he joined his hands in prayer and felt gratitude for all the beautiful elements surrounding him.

It was the season when trees and plants were fruiting or flowering. As he was marveling at the miracle of nature, Mokili noticed a colorful bird flying towards his favorite tree. He liked to pretend he was a tree. Standing with his feet together so that his body created a straight line, he shifted his weight onto his right foot, bent his left knee against his right leg and lifted his arms up.

The majestic mango tree was bearing fruit.
It was filled with clusters of big, ripe mangoes.

Mokili shifted his weight onto his right leg,
extended his arms out to the sides as if to imitate the
wings of a bird, lifting his left leg to the back,
and bending his torso forward like a plane.

As his wings opened, he switched legs all the way
to the tree to look for the juiciest, biggest mango that
he could grab. One of them was so fragrant, bright and
glowing from the warm sunrays that he exclaimed
joyfully: 'This is the one!'

The boy approached to pull the fleshy fruit from its branch. Feet closed, he lifted his arms and clasped the mango with both hands. He pulled with all his strength, bending from the left to the right.

The fruit wouldn't detach so Mokili pulled and pulled,
harder and harder.
He tried bending backwards. No matter how hard
he pulled the fruit wouldn't give in.
'Ouch!' screamed a voice. 'You are hurting me.
Stop pulling.'
'Is someone playing a trick on me?' asked Mokili.
He looked around to see if there was anyone
hiding in the nearby bushes but he saw no one.
After a lot of effort, he was tired and sweaty
so he dropped his hands towards the floor bringing
his weight into the balls of his feet.

'It's me! The mango. Please stop pulling me. It hurts.'

Lifting his head up, spine flat and pressing his
fingertips into the ground
Mokili asked the recalcitrant fruit
'Are you a magic mango?'

'No, I am not magical. All fruits, flowers, plants
and trees are living beings. We speak the
Twilight Language. It is a secret code of the heart
that humans used to know. In ancient times,
we all communicated together but this connection has been
lost as people have moved away from the wisdom of nature.'

'Why were you pulling me so hard anyway?' the fruit continued.

'Well, to eat you. What else? Isn't that what
fruits are for?', responded Mokili as he stretched
his hands to the front, bending his knees and sinking
into an imaginary chair .

'Ah! Ah! Ah!', laughed the mango. Since they
forgot the Twilight Language, humans can't hear nature.
They see her as a supermarket that they own.
They treat each and every one of us plants and animals as
lifeless objects of consumption. So often they lock us
up in fields and on farms which are like prisons
to us. We have become invisible to
humans but once we were connected in love and harmony.

I would be very happy for you to eat me but before
you do so, let me share with you some secrets
that your ancestors knew.

Sit under the shade of my
mother the tree and I will tell you more about the
fruits, vegetables and spices that you eat.'

Mokili sat on his heels, spread his knees
outward and leaned his forehead into the ground.
His arms relaxed along his body.

'My mother is more than 300 years old. She knew your mother, your grandmother, your great grandmother, your great-great grandmother. She was birthed from the seed of a mango eaten by your great-great-great grandmother. That mango came from my grandfather who was in turn a tree planted by your ancestors. Our bond is as ancient as life itself. Many generations of love exist between your family and mine.'

Mokili lifted his head up straight. He sat in a butterfly position with the soles of his feet pressed against one another close to his pelvis. His hands were wrapped around his ankles.

As he gently walked his hands forward, keeping length in his spine, he remembered family photos taken in this food forest. He recalled seeing images of his parents climbing the majestic mango tree and others showing baskets filled with mangoes ready to be turned into delicious jams. Each photograph held a beautiful memory.

As the young boy slowly stretched his legs to the front and bent forward, the mango continued:

'Food makes every part of your body, so you are literally made of what you eat. If you eat me, my flesh becomes you. You and I become one. Isn't that magical? A love union between you and me. It gives me great pleasure to nourish you and love you. I give myself to you selflessly because we are one.'

Mokili beamed in awe at the thought of being one with the beauty that is nature.

As he smiled the mango continued, 'I am made of an infinite web of life, everything collaborated perfectly to create me and consequently you. Eating me is like receiving a loving hug from all creation.'

Mokili lay down on his back and hugged his knees to his chest. He felt the embrace of all that made the mango as the fruit continued:

"I am the planets and the stars. In eating me, you are receiving blessings from the universe.

I am the sun and the moon. I absorb sunlight and moonlight to make my own food. In eating me, you are receiving the love of the sun and the moon.

I am the clouds, the rain, the oceans, and the rivers. I soak up water to keep me plump and healthy. In eating me, you are caressed and enfolded in the loving kindness of the clouds, the rain, the oceans, and the rivers.

I am the vitamin-laden soil of the earth. In eating me, you are receiving support from the land .

Mokili was filled with awe and gratitude for the benevolence of nature. Eating a fruit, a vegetable or any plant would never be the same again for him. He promised himself that, from henceforth he would treat food with respect, love and kindness.

Mokili lay on the ground. He separated his legs with his arms alongside his body, his eyes closed and his were limbs fully relaxed.

He thanked all that had come together to create his food. With that, the mango softly fell off the tree and right onto Mokili's heart.

The boy was overwhelmed with love and gratitude. To honor their sacred bond he took a bite with the gentleness of a kiss.

The mango's grace was in fact the grace of the Universe...

Swaady is one of Africa's most recognized young leaders, influencers and tastemakers. She's a former Corporate Executive and a multi-award winning entrepreneur, founder of the tea company YSWARA. Swaady is a spiritual activist and the founder of Touché Global Consciousness Summit & Events. She's an alumna of the Harvard Divinity School, an Archbishop Desmond Tutu Leadership Fellow , a certified Yoga & Mindfulness teacher for children and a certified Pranic Healer. Profiled extensively in African and global media, she has been featured on several magazine covers, received numerous recognitions including the Forbes and Oprah Winfrey O Power lists for Africa. A sought-after inspirational speaker, Swaady dreams of a world where all children are supported to explore self-knowledge so that they can build strong foundations for a happy life.

Hailing from Mumbai, India, Yogesh Mahajan has donned many hats in his field of work. He is a storybook illustrator, an animation film designer and provides many illustration services for storybooks, print, animated TV shows and mobile games to National and International clients.

His zeal and passion towards his craft clearly shows in his work.
Yogesh believes in bringing fresh and new ideas to the table for every project of his, which has made his clientele larger and loyal with time.
His EXCLUSIVE crayon art style is specially designed for kids' books.

To check out his work and know more about him,
 visit www.animationwalayogi.in .

CPSIA information can be obtained
at www.ICGtesting.com
Printed in the USA
LVHW070255230321
682155LV00003B/45